George Rockwell

Meanderings among a thousand Islands

Or, An Account of Capt. Visger's daily Trip on the River St. Lawrence

George Rockwell

Meanderings among a thousand Islands
Or, An Account of Capt. Visger's daily Trip on the River St. Lawrence

ISBN/EAN: 9783337148027

Printed in Europe, USA, Canada, Australia, Japan

Cover: Foto ©ninafisch / pixelio.de

More available books at **www.hansebooks.com**

AMONG

A THOUSAND ISLANDS,

OR AN ACCOUNT OF

CAPT. VISGER'S DAILY TRIP

ON THE

RIVER ST. LAWRENCE.

WATERTOWN, N. Y.:
TIMES AND REFORMER PRINTING AND PUBLISHING HOUSE.
1881.

THOUSAND ISLANDS,

BY THE WANDERER.

The St. Lawrence is a very monarch of rivers. The rainfalls of half a continent, gathered into the largest reservoirs of fresh water upon the earth's surface, constitute its sources of supply. The course of its stream for more than seven hundred miles, from Lake Ontario to the Gulf, where its vast volume mingles with the Ocean, lies between shores, and over soils and rocks whose character changes with almost every geological formation known. Scattered along its whole length are numerous Islands, whose varied aspects and formations, as well as the constantly changing appearance of its banks, present every variety of natural scenery to the voyager upon its waters.

That portion of the River which extends from Lake Ontario down the course of its stream for about fifty miles and which is irregularly filled up with Islands, of which the entire number is probably near two thousand, varying in size from a few feet in diameter to many miles in extent, was originally termed by the old French and Canadian voyagers

THE LAKE OF A THOUSAND ISLANDS.

It has a breadth from Kingston, in Canada, to Cape Vincent, on the American shore, the direct line being across Long or Wolfe Island, which is also about where the waters, in common parlance, begin to be designated as "the River," of about ten miles, from which it gradually though irregularly diminishes to less than one mile, where a ferry now connects the termini of railroads at the Canadian town of Brockville, and the village of Morristown on the New York side. It is this portion, perhaps more particularly the central and lower parts of it, where the Islands are more closely disposed, which has come to be designated as the "Thousand Islands of the St. Lawrence," and which has long been known and celebrated by poets and novelists for its singular and natural beauty. The wild forest, intermingled with partial cultivation upon its Islands and shores ; the many narrow and torturous channels, land-locked bays, with secluded and sheltered nooks among its several clusters, alternated with extensive stretches of open water, many of which themselves might well be called lakes, all clear and pure as the most transparent crystal, present scenes of enchantment, whose beauties are ever changing and never wearying to the eye of the beholder.

THE STEAMER "ISLAND WANDERER."

It is a region, which, while multitudes have desired to visit, and in fact of which many have caught partial glimpses in the hasty passage of the old St. Lawrence Steamers down the usually navigated channels, yet comparatively few have been able entirely to explore. The time and expense required to traverse all its multiplied channels, and the meager facilities within reach for doing so, have, until very recently, effectually concealed many of its most delightful views from the observation of the multitudes who desired to see them. Within a few years and largely by the efforts of

CAPT. E. W. VISGER,

a life long resident of the vicinity, who has constantly endeavored to extend the excursions of his Steam Yachts, many of the more interesting and less frequented localities have been brought to the delighted vision of thousands who otherwise had never come within their reach.

The very best and most satisfactory view that can possibly be obtained, in a short time, of the wonderful beauty here so lavishly displayed is undoubtedly to be had in taking an excursion on one of the trips of this Steam Yacht.

THE "ISLAND WANDERER"

Has been built and arranged with the express purpose of affording the best facilities for visiting the scenery among the Islands. While, of course, it is not pretended to pass through every channel and to give a view of every Island, or even to embrace the whole extent of all these several magnificent clusters, the trip does present in its entire compass of about forty miles, and in a general view, the more prominent features of the most interesting portions, such as is not to be had so satisfactorily in any other way. Nor in fact, is it to be obtained at all in any way, except by the employment, at large expense of

PRIVATE YACHTS.

These from their smaller sizes are able to enter the narrower channels, and so to visit the several localities in more particular detail, yet from their smaller elevation above the water fail to present the more extended panoramas, the views of which are obtained from the higher deck of the Wanderer, and very often also they occupy several days in exploring the ground traversed by her in a single trip. If one has leisure and means at command, it would undoubtedly be pleasant and interesting, after obtaining the general view of which we have spoken, to visit with smaller boats and more particularly to explore the narrower channels and more secluded nooks, occasionally taking a bass or pickerel for picnic dinner from the well known fishing grounds of which we catch the most delightful though more transient glimpses from the deck of the Wanderer.

We take it for granted that no one who visits these now celebrated Islands will wish to leave them without participating at least once (and many go made times without failure of interest) in the enjoyment of this excursion, and as it will be regarded by many persons as desirable to preserve some memento of so delightful an experience, this little account of the trip, with some local and historical information in regard to prominent places and objects of interest which it brings to view has been prepared, which in connection with the

MAP OF THE ROUTE

and the adjacent portions of the river (of which copies are for sale on the boat) will both serve the immediate purpose of giving such information as is often desired, and afterward of preserving their features in the memory of those who have enjoyed the excursion.

As the boat stops briefly at the principal summer resorts on her route among the Islands, the visitor may commence his journey at any convenient point. The time table and fares are so arranged as to give every one the entire round, and generally if desired to stop over a few hours at any of the landings between the trips and resume his journey on the return of the boat, all in one day and for a single moderate fare.

The trip proper, however, commences at the village of

ALEXANDRIA BAY,

which seems to be a sort of central headquarters for most of the various movements of the summer life among the Islands, although it is perhaps true that hundreds who have reached only some of the upper parks suppose (we think however erroneously) that they have seen the Thousand Islands, when, in fact, they have never yet set eyes on the loveliness which surrounds this most charming of all their summer resorts. For the sake then of following the entire route in regular order, we will make this our

STARTING POINT,

and begin our account with the departure of the boat from her dock in front of Cornwall Brother's stone store. I do not propose to give any lengthened description of the village and its famous hotels. This is to be found in the Hotel Guide Books, and as this little book is supposed to be in the hands of those who either have had or will have opportunity to see these for themselves, the labor of description may well be spared. Of the village itself, it may be of some interest to the curious in the local antiquarian history, to note that its site was selected so far back as 1804 by a surveyor for

JAMES LE RAY DE CHAUMONT.

This gentleman was the son of a distinguished French nobleman, and left the court of France toward the close of the last century and settled in this county. Whether or not it was in anticipation of the political troubles then brewing, and which a few years later eventuated in the bloody scenes of the French revolution, we cannot certainly say, but it is a well-known historical fact that then and soon afterward there was a very considerable French immigration to this and other points contiguous to the St. Lawrence. De Chaumont became a proprietor of extensive tracts of land in Jefferson county, and it was under his auspices that this town and others were first permanently settled. He gave his name and the names of various members of his family to many towns and villages, among them that of his son Alexander to Alexandria. He was long known as a very popular and public-spirited citizen, who not only encouraged settlement and improvement upon his own lands, but identified himself with all the interests of the country of his temporary adoption, but finally returned to his estates in France about 1810.

Alexandria Bay was chosen as the most feasible locality along this part of the river for a

PORT OF ENTRY

for a considerable section of the adjacent country, being, in fact, the only good harbor easily accessible between Clayton and Morristown, a distance of about thirty-four miles. In the very early settlement it had a considerable trade in timber and staves, of which vast quantities were collected every season in the sheltered waters on either side of the village. I have thought of this as the probable origin of the familiar cognomen by which the little settlement has been so long known. The place where the principal produce of their industry was carried to be sold or bartered was really a "bay," although which of two it would be difficult now to decide. So short and easy a title naturally transferred itself to the whole settlement, and so the village acquired the soubriquet which it seems destined now to retain. The collections of timber in various forms, were annually floated by the merchants who purchased them in large rafts to the Montreal market. Later, and in fact up to about twenty years ago, in the flourishing days of the lake navigation, before the steamboats were superseded by the railroads on either side of Lake Ontario, it was a place for large shipments of produce from the interior.

Many thousands of bushels of grain and packages of dairy products found their way to distant markets over its wharves. The cutting and gathering of wood for the supply of the Steamboats which navigated the Lake and River was also a very important industry, the activity of which for a long period gave winter employment to a considerable part of the population, and enabled many to pay for their land.

But perhaps we are dwelling too long upon upon these local memories of the past, and you will be impatient for the enjoyment of the present in the commencement of our promised excursion. We will choose the afternoon trip as the one more generally patronized from this point, and on fine afternoons, as are most of those in summer on the St. Lawrence, it will be a real luxury to get away from the hotels and breathe freely the pure ozonic air that at this hour is usually fanning the surface of the water to a gentle ripple.

Going on board a few minutes before the hour of starting, we may have a brief opportunity to gaze upon the

PANORAMA OF LIFE AND BEAUTY

which spreads around us. It may be supposed that you have not failed to notice the magnificent hotels which are just at hand, the two larger, the "Thousand Island House" and the "Crossmon," both within a few rods on either side immediately fronting, and the well kept grounds extending to the river, and the "St. Lawrence," somewhat smaller, but still able to accommodate about 100 guests, just opposite us and a block further back. While waiting for the boat to start let us take a preliminary view of

WHAT IS GOING ON ABOUT US.

The Dock itself presents a busy scene. Lusty porters sweating under the enormous loads of baggage going off in the afternoon boats for the railroads at Cape Vincent and Clayton, and parties of ladies and gentlemen hurrying to the same destination. Skiffs are gaily flitting in various directions over the river in front, some filled with parties of pleasure rowing about for their own amusement; some intent on preparations for fishing; some perhaps bringing passengers from the Islands in the vicinity, for departure by the boats, or perhaps to join the Wanderer in her favorite excursion.

THE MORE DISTANT SURROUNDINGS

may well also take a moment of our attention. Look right over the stern of our boat across the bay below Crossmon's. On the rocky point beyond is

BONNIE CASTLE,

the beautiful and unique summer residence of Dr. J. G. Holland, whose name you will at once recognize as the accomplished and talented editor of Scribner's Magazine, and one of the most celebrated of our American literary men—whom not to know something of, especially here at Alexandria Bay, for which he has done so much, and where he is so loved and honored, were a display of ignorance not lightly to be confessed. The Doctor thinks this part of the St. Lawrence, if not the most beautiful, yet "the sweetest spot on earth," and no doubt the high excellence of his literary work is largely due to the inspiration of the summer breezes which for three or four months in the year it gives him so richly to enjoy. In front of Bonnie Castle we have

AN EXTENDED AND MAGNIFICENT VIEW

down the channel of the River, which is studded with Islands that seem to float like emeralds on a sea of glass. On a few of them are small cottages, but they are too distant to be readily distinguished, and in fact for the owners of most of them we shall ourselves have to refer to the list published in connection with the map. The Sunken Rock Light House about half a mile distant, beyond which lies an Island of some forty acres in its primitive forest condition, called Deer Island, and the Canadian Light House about four miles distant on the head of a large Island known here as "Grenadier," you will not fail to see. A little to the left of these across the channel of the river, about a mile distant, but still in good view, is what is known as

MANHATTAN ISLAND,

on which are the tasteful summer residences of Judge Jas. C. Spencer, of New York city, and J. L. Hasbrouck. It it the largest and central Island of quite a little group which is known as "Manhattan group," some of which are connected by rustic bridges, and together are a little paradise. This is the first Island on which any one attempted a summer home.

SETH GREEN,

now widely known as the fish commissioner of the State of New York, built a cottage there, where his family summered and he went a-fishing for two or three seasons, about twenty-five years ago, and it is a very probable supposition that here he acquired, a part at least, of the skill in fish-ology which has since become so celebrated and useful. Glancing still around to the left we get a glimpse of a small house on elevated ground, which is on

DESHLER'S,

a beautiful Island of about fifteen acres, the property of W. G. Deshler, Esq., a banker of Columbus, Ohio, one of the early discoverers of the beauty of the Thousand Islands, who for many years has generally made Alexandria Bay his summer quarters. The little cottage is for the accommodation of the man who takes care of the Island, Mr. Deshler prefering to remain with his family at Crossmon's. Still further to the left, and above Deshler's is

HART'S ISLAND,

on the highest point of which, the tower and roof of a large and handsome cottage show themselves among the oaks which crown the summit. It was erected by the Hon. E. K. Hart, of Albion, N. Y., about 1873, but has usually for a few summers past been occupied by parties from Ogdensburg. Hart's Island is reputed as the place where the Irish poet Moore wrote the celebrated Canadian Boat Song, early in the present century. The tradition has this foundation, that the published works of Moore mention it as having been written on the St. Lawrence, as also one other of his poems, and since this establishes the fact that he visited the Islands somewhere, the song is just as likely to have been composed here as anywhere else, which is probably about all there is of it.

Away past the head of Hart's Island and quite across a larger intervening stretch of water on the other side of it, we get a view of several cottages in the forest on

WESTMINSTER PARK

which occupies five hundred acres of the lower point of Wells Island. You will also notice the long dock built for the use of the Park on this side, and some distance back from the shore, the spire of Bethune Chapel crowning the high wooded knoll where it shows itself among the forest growth. It is a pretty structure, erected by the Park Association for the use of its residents and visitors, where divine worship is observed in the usage of the Presbyterian Church during the visiting season. As opportunity will be given to call at the Park on our return homeward, a nearer and more satisfactory view of the improvements of this magnificent summer resort, which are more on the other side, may be had by any one desiring to visit them. The next in order of the circuit of the panorama before us, is a very fine summer house erected the present season (1881) for Mrs. LeConte, of Philadelphia. It is on

ISLE IMPERIAL,

which was formerly not much more than a little cluster of rocks with a few trees on one of them, but having been enlarged by filling between and around them, is so finely located in front of the hotels and but a few hundred yards distant, as to have become one of the most attractive of residences. Next in order is a small cottage on another small Island called "Maud" not much more than the size of a city lot, and the property of Rev. F. B. A. Lewis, of Watertown. Miss Bullock, of Adams, owns the cottage perched on the cliff almost dirrectly beyond, which is on a high bluff of Wells Islands well named Point Lookout, as it looks out on the most magnificent prospect in every direction, On the same Island not far above, are to be seen between the smaller Islands, some of the buildings of a large dairy farm of five hundred acres at which our cottage summer residents find it convenient to be supplied with milk during their stay. Nearly between the dairy buildings and our position

FLORENCE ISLAND

has a small tasty cottage owned by H. S. Chandler, Esq., understood to be connected with the "N. Y. Independent."

RYE ISLAND

immediately above, was cleared of its timber some years since, and some cultivation attempted upon it, but the effort to make it productive has long since been abandoned, and having partially grown up with young trees, is is a favorite camping ground for parties of young people who desire to remain in the vicinity of the village and hotels. It is still owned by Messrs. Walton, the original proprietors of all the Islands in the vicinity, who have declined for the present to dispose of it, though we believe they have had frequent opportunities of doing so at a large price.

FRIENDLY ISLAND,

which will be easily distinguished as we pass up on our course, by its name conspicuously painted on the steep abattis of rock which fronts the channel of the river just above, is owned by some gentlemen in New York city, who purchased it some years since, as was understood for purposes of improvement, which for some reason have not been effected.

In the interval between Rye and Friendly Islands, peeps out of the foliage where it is snugly nestled among embowering trees, an unpretending cottage that you would hardly observe except by close inspection. It is on

WELCOME ISLAND,

a visit to which would charm any one who loves to look out of some quiet nook upon the hurry of the busy world, and be himself undisturbed by it.   It is the property and summer residence of Hon. S. G. Pope, of Ogdensburg, whose taste and resources as a builder are amply shown in the finest structures both of simple cottages and more elaborate residences which grace the Islands of the vicinity.

Above Welcome and Friendly Islands and in full view are the white cottages of

PULLMAN ISLAND,

which although by no means pretentious in its architectural erections, yet from its associations is probably an object of quite as general interest as any in the vicinity.   It is the property of Geo. M. Pullman, Esq., of Sleeping Car notoriety, whose entertainment of Gen. Grant with a large party of friends in the summer of 1872 has so impressed itself among the notable events of the Islands as not soon to be forgotten.

THE VISIT OF THE PRESIDENT OF THE U. S.

a notable event at any time, was especially so as it occurred the summer preceeding the presidential election which gave Gen. Grant his second term of office, and was of course a matter of interest throughout the country.   The political caldron was boiling with all the activity incident to the near election, and multitudes of patriotic citizens, to say nothing of aspiring politicians all over the country suddenly discovered how exceeding pleasant, convenient and conductive to health it might be to visit the St. Lawrence and go-a-fishing, for what? may easily be conjectured.   But this visit, whether or not it had anything to do with the next presidency, evidently had a great deal to do in directing public attention to the Islands as a delightful and accessible summer resort, and it probably lost none of its natural effect upon the public mind from the circumstance that a large party of members of the newspaper press, on an excursion from Watertown, where they were in attendance on an editoral convention, had been very handsomely entertained at an out door collation on the same Island, early the same season.

There had for some years been a plentiful lack of accommodation for any very large number who might desire to spend some time at the Islands. This year the lack, greater than ever, was demonstrated in a very practical way. As the immediate result, plans for new and larger hotels, long before talked of, found active promoters with the necessary amount of capital. The next season these two immense caravanseries were ready for the reception of guests, and since that time Alexandria Bay has been famous. Changes and improvements have since been continually going on, all looking particularly to the accommodation of the increasing thousands who have here annually sought health and recreation.

. But by this time the boat will be starting—we shall soon see more evidences of the improvements of which we speak. As we pass up the River the first to claim our attention is a very neat cottage, or rather two of them, on a little cliff, which emerged from their hiding behind Friendly Island on the right. They are on

NOBBY ISLAND,

NOBBY ISLAND.

the property of Henry R. Heath, of New York city, and C. E. Goodwin, of Oneida, N. Y., who built here about 1873, and who with their many friends have made the Island merry with their annual gatherings.

CHERRY ISLAND

on the left, had a small rough cottage erected upon it, as early as 1860, which has been variously and irregularly occupied, mainly as a convenient shelter for camping parties. This year there have been two other and better cottages built, the first, a large house named "Melrose Lodge, by parties from Chicago, socially connected with the Pullmans. In fact the wife of A. B. Pullman, Esq., with her friend Mrs. G. B. Marsh, are joint owners. The upper and smaller cottage is owned by Rev. Geo. Rockwell, now of Fulton, N. Y., but best known in this region as for more than twenty years the pastor of the Reformed Church, the first organized in Alexandria Bay.

Nearly opposite this we pass quite near Pullman Island. Just above Cherry Island you mark the singular Rock known as Oven Island, or as some call it

"DEVIL'S OVEN,"

which rises out of the deep water much in the general form of an

old fashioned out door Dutch oven, and to complete the resemblance, has a large opening at the water level under one side, which is said to have been one of the hiding places of the celebrated Bill Johnston, who figured largely hereabout in the border troubles of 1837-38, the scene of whose most famous exploit we will pass by and by.

Above the oven we pass on the left four cottages, two of which we can only name as Cuba, owned by W. F. Story, built about 1876, and Wau Winet, by J. G. Hill, of Chicago, built last year.

WARNER'S ISLAND

is the third, and is situated about in the centre of the channel, so that we pass quite near, and get a good view of the improvements. It is the property of H. H. Warner, a wealthy and public spirited citizen of Rochester, N. Y., whose name ought to be pretty well known, at least in this vicinity seeing that his "Safe Bitters," "Safe Pills," "Safe Tonic," "Safe Kidney Cure" and other "Safe" medicines are not sparingly advertised, not only in the newspapers generally, but especially hereabout on buildings, fences, and other convenient sign boards, almost everywhere except on his own Island. Whatever we may think of the taste or utility of his advertisements, we cannot deny that Mr. Warner has shown excellent taste in choosing and adorning his summer home, for he has here transformed what was before rather a barren and rocky island to a garden of beauty and attraction.

WARNER'S ISLAND.

Just above Warner's we pass the twin Islands, Pratt and Centennial, on the upper of which Mr. H. Sisson, of Alexandria Bay, has built a little cottage. All along on our right, from Pullman's Island up, we have been passing near the shore of Wells Island, which, though rock bound, and in some places somewhat precipitous to some fifty or sixty feet in height, is covered generally with quite a considerable native forest growth. The whole frontage is understood to have been sold not long since by Mr. Sisson to parties who contemplate improvement but whose work has been carried no further than a little cleaning up of underbrush, and encouraging the proper growths. The range is terminated by a miniature "Anthony's nose" of bare rock marked "Louisiana Point" purchased a few years since by the Hon. Judge Labatte, of New Orleans, while on a visit here, with a purpose of a summer home. In a little bay immediately above are a few acres of smoother land, most of which is very prettily shaded, which has been laid out and mapped in small lots and designated

"EMERALD PARK,"

and which are understood to be held for sale by Mr. Sisson, at low rates, for the convenience of those who do not desire, or whose means do not permit the occupation of an entire island.

Immediately above, and apparently adjoining, was originally a low island of a few acres, intersected with marsh, but having been improved by digging out the marsh, has been separated into a cluster of small Islets and called

SEVEN ISLES.

These are all covered with a young growth which bids fair to become the loveliest of groves, shading all the narrow channels. A small cottage, half hid among them, is owned, as in fact is the whole cluster, by Hon. B. Winslow, of Watertown, now a member of the State senate from this district.

In Densmore Bay, above, and some distance to the right, McIntyre the photograph man, who makes pictures of all the islands and parties who desire them, has a little home cottage and picture factory, which he properly enough denominates

"PHOTO."

There are also farm houses and farms now on both sides, those on the right hand being on Wells Island, the left the main shore, but it is hardly necessary to do more than to call your attention to the patience and economy necessary to dig a living among these rocks. Evidently these shores are not calculated to compete in corn and wheat cultivation with the prairies of the west. Nevertheless these farmers do contrive to live very comfortably, principally off the products of the dairy, as what land there is, not entirely unfertile, is best adapted for grazing.

POINT VIVIAN.

About a mile above Warner's Island on the main, is a little cluster of twelve or fifteen cottages which will attract attention. They have been built mostly by residents of the interior of Jefferson county for the convenience of spending a few weeks of the warm season on the river. They purchased this wooded point, and have built each to please himself, and so form a little neighborhood where each has an independent home, but yet in the society of his friends.

For the next two or three miles nothing needful of special note is presented. The channel is usually quite contracted, and in fact has the local name of the "Narrows" but it irregularly sends off the branching bays on both sides some of which are hidden behind jutting points. The most beautiful of these, about thirty acres of excellent land, being but slightly bordered with rock, and covered with the original very beautiful forest growth, long known as "Page Point," and latterly called Grinnell Park, from its ownership by a gentleman of that name, is understood to have recently changed hands along with a considerable farm adjoining, and is soon to be, if it is not already, opened under the name of

"CENTRAL PARK"

for the building of cottages and summer residences. Near its western extremity a long low building has been sometimes opened as a boarding house, and has this year been enlarged.

Less than a mile above this, a very cosy summer house on a half acre Island at the left is the property of Rev. Henry G. Waite, formerly U. S. Consul to Rome; now understood to be engaged in literary work in connection with some periodical publication in N. Y. city, who generally makes a visit of a few weeks, with family and friends. He calls the Island

Shortly above Collins Landing the narrow channel begins to widen, and a number of farm houses, with a factory for Limberger cheese on the Wells Island side, somewhat vary the landscape. While the shore of Wells continues rocky, the farms on the main are now more extended and the land generally susceptible of cultivation. About half a mile above the cheese factory on Wells Island, is the

PEEL DOCK

so called from the destruction of the steamer Sir Robert Peel, a well remembered incident of the border troubles of 1837-8, to which allusion has already been made. Not to enter at length into the history of those troubles, it may be sufficient to say that an abortive attempt to revolutionize the Canadas, generally known as the Patriot war, found many sympathizers and awakened great interest all along the border. The burning of the American steamer Caroline near Niagara by a band of men from Canada, while it aroused a general indignation throughout the States, especially intensified the excitement here, and produced a feeling difficult to repress. Men were enlisted, and organizations effected who threatened and in fact attempted an invasion of Canada in the interest of those who desired revolution. The particulars of the burning of the Peel are thus related by Mr. Hough in his history of Jefferson county:

On the night between the 29th and 30th of May, 1838. the British steamer Sir Robert Peel, was plundered and burned at Wells Island, under the following circumstances. * * * * She was on her way from Prescott to Toronto, with nineteen passengers, and had left Brockville in the evening, which was dark and rainy, and arrived at McDonald's wharf, on the south side of Wells Island, in the town of Clayton, at midnight, for the purpose of taking on wood.

Threats of violence had been intimated, and before the steamer had left Brockville, it was hinted to one on board that there was danger of an attack, but this threat was not regarded. The passengers were asleep in the cabin and the crew had been engaged about two hours in taking on wood, when a company of twenty-two men, disguised, and painted like savages, and armed with muskets and bayonets, rushed on board, yelling and shouting, "remember the Caroline!" drove the passengers and crew to the shore, allowing but a hasty opportunity for removing a small part of the baggage, and toward morning, having cast the boat into the stream, to about thirty rods distance, set it on fire. The scene of confusion and alarm which this midnight attack occasioned among the passengers can be better imagined than described.

Some of them fled to the shore in their night-clothes, and a considerable portion of the baggage was lost. After the boat was fired in several places, a party including Thomas Scott a passenger, (a surgeon who had stayed to dress a wound) got into two long boats and started for Abel's Island, four miles from Wells Island, where they arrived about sunrise. He stated that there were twenty-two persons besides himself and the wounded man, in the two boats. The brigands were known to each other by fictitious names, as Tecumsah. Sir William Wallace, Judge Lynde, Capt. Crockett, Nelson, Captain Crocker, Bolivar and Admiral Benbo. Several thousand dollars in one package, and also smaller sums, were taken from the boat and various articles of clothing. The only house in the vicinity of the wharf was the woodman's shanty, where the passengers found refuge until five o'clock in the morning, when the Oneida, Capt. Smith, came down on her regular trip, and finding the distressed situation of the unfortunate persons returned with them to Kingston. It is. said to have been the intention of those who took the Peel, to have captured with her aid the steamer Great Britian the next day, and to have cruised with these steamers on the lake, and transport troops and supplies for the patriot service.

The leader of this outrage was William, or as he was commonly called "Bill Johnson," well known on the border for his bitter hatred of the English and Canadian governments, and ready for any measure that might aid the so called "patriot" cause. So far from denying, it appears that he rather gloried in the exploit. Of course it at once not only awakened the indignation of Canada, but aroused our own government to the necessity of guarding the frontier and preventing a breach with the Canadian authorities. Gov. Marcy, then in the executive chair of New York, himself visited Jefferson County and took measures to repress any further hostile demonstration. A large reward was offered by our own,

and a larger by the Canadian executive, for the arrest of the out-
laws, and the officials of both countries united in the effort for
their capture, especially of Johnson. It has, however, been hinted
that the American detail professedly engaged in this service, did
not lose a great deal of necessary sleep by their watchfulness.
Johnson was aided, in his hiding among the Islands, by his
daughter, it is said in a boy's disguise. As she was then a very
attractive young woman, a spice of romance for a long time attach-
ed to her adventures, and her fame as the "Queen of the Isles"
extended through the whole region. The writer met her many
years since at Clayton, where she was married and the mother of
a family, who, so far as discovered, bore no especial marks of
royal birth. She is, we believe, now dead, but some of Johnson's
sons are living in Clayton.

Late in the fall he was arrested by the American authorities,
but escaped, and was re-arrested two or three times, until finally
the border having become quiet, he returned to Clayton and was
no more molested. Indeed, so far from the American government
having any continued desire for his punishment, he seemed to
meet with favor, and as probably a good democrat, was appointed
by the administration of President Pierce, keeper of the light at
Rock Island, which shines on the very spot where the Peel was
burned. The explanation is believed to be that he had before
rendered effectual, though perhaps not very reputable service, to
the U. S. in the war of 1812, when employed as a spy, he had suc-
ceeded in plundering the British mails of important despatches
which he brought to the American officers at Sackets Harbor; and
this explanation has the color of plausibility, as it is said he was
appointed by the recommendation of Gen. Scott, who, as an officer
of the American army, was during that war engaged in the military operations then in progress upon the frontier, and probably
knew all about Johnson's services.

But to return to the description of our trip. Not far above the
Peel dock we come to some recent improvements upon a cluster of
small Islands, and on the shore of Wells, that have incidently
grown out of the location of the Thousand Island Park, which we
are now rapidly approaching. We cannot particularize them all.
On the small Islands at the left are several summer residences of
various sizes and pretensions. The nearest, "Frederick Island,"
is owned by a gentleman of that name, a merchant in Carthage, N.
Y. The second "Occident and Orient," by a N. Y. gentleman
named Washburn. The third is an expensive house belonging to

E. N. Robinson, a broker, who has been somewhat noted for large operations in Wall street, where it is said he has both made and lost sums of money reaching into the millions, very rapidly. There are some two or three more distant cottages on Islands whose names and owners are in the list and map we use. Over back of these Islands is a little hamlet known as

FISHER'S LANDING,

where a very comfortable house called the "Central Hotel" entertains, in a quiet way, a good many summer guests. On the Wells Island side we pass some clusters of cottages and one hotel, the "Wellesley House," before reaching the Park proper, for the names of whose owners we again refer to the lists on the map, at "Jolly Oaks" and "Waving Branches." As we turn to the right to make our landing at the Thousand Island Park, we pass the Rock Island Light House, which guards the navigator against several surrounding dangerous rocks and indicates the proper entry from the open water above into the narrower channels we have been ascending. Some two or three miles distant across the intervening stretch of open water above, and nearly in the centre of a large level Island, a large building somewhat resembling the Thousand Island House at Alexandria Bay, looms conspicuously into view. It is the

ROUND ISLAND HOTEL

and Round Island, of some eighty acres, is laid out as a park around it. Could we visit it we should find many exceedingly pretty cottages lining its shores. It was purchased about two years since and is conducted nominally in the interest of the Baptist denomination. It is about two miles this side of the village of Clayton, which it hides from our view, and being easy of access from the railroad at that point is quite a favorite resort for the denomination named and many others. Capt. Visger has often been importuned to extend his trip so as to make it one of the stopping places of the "Wanderer," but its situation will not permit his doing so without sacrificing more time than can well be spared from the remainder of the trip.

THOUSAND ISLAND PARK.

Here the boat makes a stop of several minutes, and we have time to land and walk a little about the Park if desired. A small admission fee of ten cents is, we believe, charged at the gate. But to get a satisfactory view of the Park it would have been better to have come up on the morning trip and wait over, as many do, resuming the excursion in the afternoon.

We need say but a few words of this park, which has become one of the summer institution, of the country, and has already been visited by thousands, both from Canada and the U. S. It had its beginning in the winter of 1874-5, although by the invitation of its projector, Rev. J. F. Dayan, parties of ministers and others, chiefly members of the Methodist Episcopal Church, had the autumn before visited various localities of the Islands within a radius of several miles for the purpose of selecting a site. The upper end of Wells Island, on the American side, was finally chosen and arrangements informally commenced for its purchase. With considerable negotiation, and some hesitation in regard to the quantity of land needed for the success of the enterprise, the projectors, who had during the winter effected an organization as the "Thousand Island Camp Meeting Association," finally purchased all the land in the neighborhood then open to sale, (about 950 acres) and employed an engineer to lay it out suitably for the purposes they intended it to serve. Reserving a strip all around the shore, and other grounds for the public uses, a considerable space was marked off in avenues and lots, which were offered for sale the following Spring. By this time a dock for steamers, and various buildings for boarding hall, office, stores and some lodging rooms to be owned and controlled by the association, were in good progress. By active effort, and extensive advertising, the project sprang into success at once. Lots were immediately and largely taken. Provision was made by the trustees for a series of meetings at which the ablest speakers, on religious and philanthropic subjects were to be heard. Soon not only the lots on the Park itself, but all the desirable shore property near, with the small Islands in the near vicinity, advanced largely in price and found eager buyers. Thousands became visitors, hundreds purchasers, and very many builders, so that there soon arose a considerable summer village, perhaps averaging a thousand or fifteen hundred inhabitants for two months in the year, and often increased to more than double that number on the days of especial interest in the meetings held. There are now probably more than two hundred buildings on the grounds most of which are private cottages. Some friction, of course, has occurred in the management, and some grumbling at the strictness of regulations made, or believed to be necessary for the preservation of good order upon the grounds, but on the whole the institution has had a large success. It is, however, understood that this year there is a change in the management, and that still greater effort is to be made for continuance of growth. A comfortable and commodious hotel, whose want has been greatly felt and often expressed by those that were dissatisfied with the rather primitive accommodations hitherto provided, and who were willing to pay for better, is now to be erected and other improvements looking to permanency and comfort. Hitherto the whole Park has been practically but a sort of mammoth out-door hotel, where most of the guests took meals at the boarding hall, but very generally looked after their own lodgings in cottages and tents. Still, rooms were to a limited extent provided in the upper lofts of some of the buildings, and at the same time, many families lived and had all arrangements for providing the table in their own cottage and tent homes.

Our stay at the Park is limited to a few minutes, and after receiving probably a large addition to the number of her passengers, the Wanderer moves on her way. Any further information in relation to the Park is, if desired, easily accessible in some of the publications issued in its interest, notably in a little book entitled "The Thousand Island Park, its Origin and Progress," which may probably be found at the Book Stands, and perhaps also on the boat.

From the Park Dock we move around the upper end of the Island, and you will not fail to notice the beautiful situation and ornamentation of some of the cottages nearest the river bank, along whose rocky but yet beautiful and level plateau shore, we pass to our next landing which is the

HUB HOUSE.

This is a fair sized hotel only a few rods distant from the Park, and occupying rather more than the original whole of the Rocky Hub on one side of which it is built. A few rods back and above we see Grenell's. It is on a small Island, originally a spur, but now separated from the larger one above, which is also owned and to some extent farmed by Mr. Grenell, who has resided here for many years, giving entertainment to a few guests perhaps in the rather primitive style of a country tavern. One or two cottages perched on high points of the larger Island may be found on the list in connection with our map.

Leaving the Hub House the boat swings around to the left to pass up the channel between what is marked on our map after the old charts as "Stuart," but which has been known as "Jeffers" and now commonly as Grinnell's Island from the name of the owner.

This constant change of the names of Islands is to be regretted as leading to great confusion. But it goes rapidly on, especially with the smaller Islands, which, with every change of ownership, are apt to be baptized with new names to suit the taste of the new owners. But this is not all, nor the worst. Many of the larger Islands are given names on the charts published by authority of the English and American governments, entirely different from those in common use. This has an illustration in the Islands just about us. That on the left is named on the English charts "Stuart," which was copied on the map in common use and also on the American charts. The early deeds named it "Jeffers," by which it seems once to have been generally known. So of the Island on our right. It is on the charts, both English and American, as "Murray," but hereabout is universally called "Hemlock Island." It is doubtful now if any one living in the vicinity should hear of either "Stuart" or "Murray" Island he would know what was meant.

Quite a lively controversey arose a few years since as to the proper name of "Wells Island." It is marked on the charts "Wellesley" and on the map by both names. When the Methodist people inaugurated the Park, "Wellesley" had never been heard of in the vicinity. The publisher of the map, which was first issued the same season which opened the Park, and which was based on a copy of the old English charts, in this, as in several instances, inserted both names. With the names only as given in the chart, the map would have been of very little value, for no one here knew anything about them. But when the Park began to be talked of, some astute Methodist brother discovered that Wesley was a contraction of Wellesley, and of course for a Methodist Park that would be the right name for the Island, and great efforts were made to bring the longer name into use, much to the disgust of the older inhabitants. They had received title to their lands as "being and situate on Wells Island," and had no notion of giving up the title either to farm or Island, especially for a jaw-breaking name like that proposed. A good deal of discussion arose in the newspapers and otherwise as to the proper designation, but in the vicinity and among the residents at least, the new name is *no go*. But, say the Park people, "it is the old name. the charts all have it, and no chart has the name Wells Island." The facts seem to be these.

So long ago as 1810 or 1812, before the Islands were finally divided between Canada and the U. S., one William Wells, a resident of Brockville, was engaged in lumbering on this Island, and as is generally the case in new countries, it took the name of its first occupant, and came to be known, as it always since has been in the neighborhood, as "Wells Island," and all the deeds of lands upon it are located by this name. The original patent of the Islands to Elisha Camp in 1823, did not mention any of the Islands by name, but simply conveyed all the Islands belonging to the State of New York, lying between certain designated points on the River. Upon a very old map in the possession of Messrs. Cornwall & Walton, of Alexandria Bay, which they received with an early purchase of lands upon Wells Island, and all the other small Islands lying between certain defined points, and which is said to have been made for the Commissioners of the U. S. who run and established the boundary line, this is designated "Wells Island." The date of the map is lost or omitted, but it is believed to be about 1820.*

The history and authority of the name "Wellesley" is believed to be simply this. About 1817 or 1818 an English officer, Capt. W. F. W. Owen, R. N., surveyed the River, presumably by the authority of the British Government, and a chart was made by him on which were inserted names upon many points which, with a few exceptions, had not been before known or heard of. This is evident from the fact that many of them were memorials of the European wars, in which the English had recently been engaged. Some were adopted from places where important events had transpired, others from officers who had become distinguished. Now Capt. Owen had of course some show of right in giving such names as he pleased, so far as the English side of the boundary was concerned, but it may be questioned how far it was suitable or in the best taste to apply them upon American territory, without regard to the commonly used designation of the inhabitants. But he did so very extensively, of which this is an example. Wellesley being the family name of the Duke of Wellington, the hero of Waterloo, which by the way is commemorated in the immediate vicinity, the beautiful and significant name of the "Lake of the Island," as applied to

---

*This map is entitled, "A map of all the Islands of the River St. Lawrence within the State of New York," and is in two large sheets, evidently made with great care, and each sheet signed, "Wm. A. Bird." It is much dilapidated by age and use, having been used through several extended law suits. It evidently covered originally all the Islands patented to Camp in this part of the River, which were those between Morristown and the most westerly point of Grindstone Island.

the land-bound and secluded sheet which lies, as it were, in the bosom of this very Island and is about five-sixths surrounded by its shores, is on the chart changed to "Lake Waterloo." It is to be regretted that the U. S. officers charged with the American lake survey, of which the charts of this part have been recently published, have in so many instances followed this unauthorized English nomenclature to the exclusion of names locally much better known. "Wells" is and was for years known and used in the whole region, while "Wellesley" was never heard of in the vicinity till about the time the Thousand Island Park was inaugurated, when it was brought into notice by a copy of one of the sheets of the English charts, which was borrowed and used by the gentlemen interested while engaged in canvassing for the beginnings of their enterprise, and is the same that afterward became the foundation for the very little map which has been so much used by visitors. But we are for a while about to lose sight of Wells Island, and it is a fit time to dismiss this wearisome discussion about the name into which we have been led by a desire to get the facts fully before the public, which we believe has not before been done.

As we pass up the channel between Grenell's, or Jeffers, or Stuart Island, whichever you choose to call it, and Hemlock or Murray, (you see names are as plenty as the Islands) away to the right is the

CLIFF HOUSE

another small Summer Hotel, built on a high bluff at the foot of the Island last mentioned. It is kept by Mr. E. Garrettson, formerly of the Globe Hotel in Syracuse, and is generally well patronized in the summer by guests from the Central City. Our route lies up near enough to the Island to catch a good view of some cottages along its shore, for the names of whose owners we must again refer you to the list before mentioned. Through much of this passage the village of Clayton is in full view, being about three miles distant, but we soon loose sight of it as we turn short to the right, enter a narrow gap between Hemlock and Robbins Islands, and emerge into Eel Bay, an expanse of water some three miles in diameter, with only a few low Islands, which do not interrupt the view quite to the wooded shores of another part of Wells Island again. Our way lies pretty close along the eastern shore of one of the largest of the Thousand Islands, being about four or five miles long by two and a half wide, having on it some 200 inhabitants, who reside on farms in a fair state of cultivation, and are enabled to furnish a considerable amount of supplies for the consumption of visitors. Passing around its northerly point, which is an immense naked hill, bordered by a few trees toward Canada, we speedily enter

CANADIAN WATERS

which open to our view a great stretch studded with Islands and divided into channels in a manner to bewilder any attempt to enumerate or arrange them. Hardly any of them seem to be more than a few acres in extent. Though generally rocky, they are nearly all more or less wooded, even rocks with scarce standing room for a man often supporting a tree or a bush to which he might cling in case of shipwreck. Some, however, bear evident witness of the destructive ravages of fire, which has often and sadly marred their original beauty. It evidently now

REQUIRES SKILL TO GUIDE THE COURSE OF OUR CRAFT.

Many channels open in every direction, but only the skilful pilot knows in which of them it is safe to venture. Hidden rocks abound. Some indeed reveal their position near the surface, when on a very fair day, their light brown clouds the clear green of the deeper water, but others lie further down, and all the more dangerous, because, though unseen, they are still within reach of our keel. But our pilot never hesitates. He only keeps a keen eye on the land marks, knowing that in the right channels there is generally more than a hundred feet of water between us and the bottom. Passing through some five or six miles of such navigation, sometimes almost shut up in the narrow passages, and again crossing wide stretches that are on every side broken and bounded by Islands, turning now to the right, and anon to the left as quickly, we wind torturously among the changing channels sometimes within a few feet of the rocky shore, until finally after a seeming exceedingly narrow escape from wreck upon a jutting point, we cross a not very wide passage opening eastward to an extensive bay, and make our landing at the Canadian town of Gananoque of whose steeples we have for some time caught occasional glimpses between the Islands.

GANANOQUE

is the nearest Canadian town of any size, to the great body of the Thousand Islands. It is nearly opposite and about five miles in a direct line from Clayton, and ten or twelve from Alexandria Bay, though it requires a ferriage of nearly double that distance from either, on account of the winding passage made necessary by intervening Islands. It is situated at the mouth of a river bearing the same name, which was the original natural discharge for a considerable number of small lakes lying some miles to the Northward. The Rideau Canal, which joins the St. Lawrence at Kingston with the Ottawa, diverts the water from some of them for the use of its higher levels, so that the stream is probably not so large as it would be if it received all that naturally belonged to it. It is, however, still sufficient for moving a considerable amount of machinery, which is employed for flouring and saw mills and also for various purposes of manufacture, chiefly of nails, agricultural implements, furniture and various hardware supplies. The dam which gives the fall is situated in the village, above which the stream is navigable for skiffs, with only one other portage, fifteen or twenty miles to some of the lakes which are its sources of supply. As these abound with fish and game they are often visited by sportsmen from the American side, who report the lakes to be of great beauty, and the sport, both in hunting and fishing, excellent.

Gananoque has a population of about three thousand inhabitants, with five churches of different denominations. There are several hotels where sportsmen on the river occasionally stop, as the fishing in front is said to be the best in the St. Lawrence, but there has been no sustained effort to direct attention to it, as a place of summer resort, and the sportsmen who frequent its waters are mostly in parties from Clayton, Alexandria Bay and other places on the American side. The Grand Trunk Railroad passes and has a station about two and one-half miles North of the town, but the principal business access has hitherto been by the Steamboats navigating Lake Ontario, which call here on the passage up or down the river.

LEAVING GANANOQUE

our course is at first over a considerable stretch of open water, across which the Gananoque channel, so called, is marked by a light house and beacon, known as "Jack Straw." These serve both to mark hidden shoals and as a guide for the egress of the navigator across, and out of the apparently land-locked sheet of water which stretches away on both sides. After passing between the light and beacon, our boat leaves the usual channel, which we can see marked by another light off to the right, and plunges into the depth of

HALSTED'S BAY,

where seemingly there is no way, and which is to all appearances completely shut in. When after passing dangerously near some small rocky inlets, we seem within a few rods of landing upon a low rocky point directly in front, a sudden turn to the right opens a straight but narrow estuary along which we obtain a clear view a mile or more directly ahead. What had before appeared in a solid mass as a continuous point of the main land, melts into an Island cluster, among which, as we progress, we catch glimpses of varied and intricate channels in every direction. From the contracted channel along which we now sail, other passages open and mingle in a labyrinth seemingly almost interminable. Once almost grazing a round rock that rises on our left much in the shape of a hay-cock and not much larger, we almost instinctively listen for the shock of the boat striking as she passes. But our course is straight on, though in a channel often exceedingly narrow but almost as direct as a surveyors line, till finally emerging from a strait between two high rocks, where one could easily toss a pebble to either shore, we enter the more open and usual channel where a sharp turn to the left shows us a light house about two miles ahead, a wide stretch of water dotted with Islands all about, but no visible opening through the forest covered, rock bound land, which to all appearance completely blocks the way. Wells Island lies at the right, the Canadian main at the left, on both of which a few scattered farm houses and fenced fields betoken partial cultivation. Just before reaching the light house a little cluster of Islands appear on the right, and just past these the shore of Wells Island rapidly recedes, and appears to meet the land from below at an exceeding rocky and precipitous part near the end of a narrow bay. No definite opening is here visible, in that direction, but a reference to the map shows a narrow passage, which is really not more than a man's long leap across. It is the

INLET TO THE LAKE OF THE ISLAND,

down which the water rushes with a current sufficient to turn a

 mill, which might there be built with one end each in Canada and the State of New York, and not be a very large mill either.— The magnificent cluster in front and on both sides is considered one of the finest, if not the very finest in the St.

Lawrence. The islands are generally well wooded, and you will think them gems of the best water. The entire Canada water at this point is not much more than a mile in breadth, and gradually contracts for about one and a half miles, and in that space are about eighty Islands, some of which are of considerable size, and in partial cultivation. They seem as if placed here for the express purpose of damming the stream and disputing the passage of the water, which however finds its way in many narrow and intricate passages, generally with a rapid current, to the open water below. From the broad channel in which we have been sailing, we enter a narrow pass of troubled waters, between the beetling bluffs of "Ash Island" and Lyndoc light house, situate on a small Island of not more than one acre. Our way is for a short space between these almost perpendicular rocks crowned with forrest growth on one side, and Islands of the greenest and freshest foliage on the other. A little white cottage, the residence of the light keeper, shows itself like an apparition and vanishes like magic. We catch glimpses of little spots of beauty which change and are renewed like the pictures of a kaleidoscope. A mile of such sailing from the light house, and the boat swings again to the right and enters a narrow strait, whence for a moment she emerges at the end of a broad sheet, bounded by Islands which are covered by a forest growth of the greenest verdure, but only immediately with another sharp turn in the contrary direction to enter with the seething current into another and narrower strait, where you are almost startled with the appearance of a little Island right under the bow, past which the water is rushing as from a broken mill dam. This is the vicinity of the

FIDDLER'S ELBOW

probably so called from the sudden and rapid turns necessary to its navigation, and is probably more celebrated for its marvelous loveliness than any other portion of the St. Lawrence. Its numerous and intricate channels and hidden recesses are only known to the most experienced boatmen and fishermen. Capt. Visger we perceive has given this particular part of his trip the name of the

LOST CHANNEL.

What particular private information the Capt. may possess of its former navigation is more than we are able to divine. The only record of its use, which, after long research, we have discovered is in the account of the celebrated voyage of Capt. Jasper Western, who must have passed through it in the noted expedition of the "Scud," from Oswego, for the relief of the log fort that was hidden among the Islands as far back as the time of the Pathfinder in the old French war, for the particulars of which, with the account of its discovery and capture by a party of Indians under the renowned French Captain, Mons. Sanglier, we refer to the most interesting and romantic histories of the life of Leather-stocking, the border scout, written by Mr. Fennimore Cooper. It will be remembered by those familiar with those most veracious chronicles that after the re-capture, which was successfully effected by the skill of the Pathfinder, aided by the prompt re-appearance of Capt. Western in the "Scud," the fort was abandoned and the military defences destroyed, as no longer of value. It is of course to be inferred that at the same time all knowledge of the proper approaches was purposely lost, and we surmise it has never since been discovered till Capt. Visger in his zeal for exploration of all the hidden recesses of the Islands for the delectation of his passengers, searched it out in his steam yacht, the "Wanderer." It is almost certain that the block-house fort must have been somewhere in this vicinity, from the very sufficient reason that no other is so admirably adapted to the purpose for which it was built, and no other has ever been discovered, and here it is certain that neither the French Captain nor even his Indian allies would ever have found it but for the rascally treachery of Lieutenant Muir, an English officer who accompanied the expedition with the real design of betraying it to the French, but covered his nefarious purpose with the pretense of making love to Mabel Dunham, the pretty daughter of the Sergeant in command of the party. It is to be regreted that no amount of research has yet discovered the ruins of the log fort, or exactly identified the spot where these notable events transpired, and it is hereby suggested that a promising field is here opened for the labors of amateur antiquarians, where more minute researches might be as amply rewarded as were those of Jonathan Oldenbuck in his famous explorations of the Kaim of Kinprunes.*

As we emerge from the cluster of the "Fiddler's Elbow" we come into view of Grenadier Island Light House, the same seen at Alexandria Bay before starting. A few houses and fences are to be seen upon the shore of "La Rue," the large Canadian Island at the right, but the main, which is now visible on the left, is high and in many places precipitous. Only a single house with a dock on which is piled wood, ready corded, for sale to passing steamers, relieves the almost unbroken wilderness shore. Just below this, which is Darling's wharf, the Capt., if the day is sufficiently quiet, will let you hear a

VERY DISTINCT AND DISTANT ECHO

produced evidently by the return of the sound of his whistle from the perpendicular rock just opposite.

Along down this usual Canadian channel, past both La Rue and Club Islands, some signs are manifest of the cultivation of the land in small patches between the rocks on both sides of us. Swinging short around the foot of Club Island, in front of a little Canadian hamlet very appropriately named Rockport, we soon leave Canadian waters, and catch a view of several cottages and the Hotel on

---

*Note. We are most happy to announce to the sight seeing public, that Capt. Visger has promised that no pains shall be spared in searching out the precise locality of the ruins above referred to, and that when found it shall certainly be brought within the route of his Steamer, and not only distinctly marked on every map, but particularly pointed out to every passenger who takes the least interest in identifying it.

WESTMINSTER PARK,

at whose dock we make our last landing before returning to Alexandria Bay. The name is at once suggestive of something Presbyterian, but we can assure the reader that there is nothing unpleasantly "blue" about this Park. The association was formed principally by gentlemen in sympathy with the Presbyterian church, but its gates are always freely wide open to every one. The organization was formally effected and land purchased in September, 1877, and during the fall of that year work was commenced in clearing and opening avenues through the dense forest growth which covered a large part of the grounds. Lots were laid out, and a considerable number sold in the spring of 1878, at which time a hotel was erected and the Park opened to public use. Its growth has not been so rapid as that of the Thousand Island Park, having lacked the concentration and energy of denominational purpose which characterized the other. Whether it is because Presbyterians have not the push and energy, and combined effort, and shouting power of their Methodist brethren, or because they are naturally slower and more conservative, we do not pretend to decide. Little effort has ever been made here in the way of inaugurating meetings, and bringing noted speakers to draw the crowds, only a Sunday school convention for a week having been held in 1879. The trustees have rather sought to make it a place where individuals and families who desire may find and enjoy a quiet home, with abundant room to ramble, or ride through the extensive avenues for which purpose carriages are at hand for those who desire to use them.

The grounds have been opened but just sufficiently to develop the possibilities of the future. They afford views of forest and water in every conceivable variety, and on the higher points, of great extent. The growth has been considerable, solid, and of good material, but from the great extent of the grounds is not so obvious at a single glance as if the improvements were more concentrated. Some fine cottages and residences have been built, which with the Park House, generally accommodate a population of several hundreds during the summer months. This year several cottages have been built or are in course of construction on prominent points some of which are large and expensive. The trustees have large faith that this is yet to be *the Park* of the Thousand Islands. In its natural features, and the great variety of its surface and scenery it is thought by some much to resemble the great Central Park of New York city, but the large circuit of its water boundary and the greater height of its eminences, and rocky precipices, with the great extent and variety of its natural forest growth, give it the advantages of mingled and various views of land, water and foliage nowhere else to be seen except among the Thousand Islands of the St. Lawrence. While the boat lies a few minutes at the wharf, we may call at the Park House, stroll about some of the nearest avenues, and so get a glimpse of some of the cottages embowered among the trees, but fully to explore them all, needs a day, or at least several hours, when as we walk or ride, each new turn will reveal new and differing phases of natural loveliness.

Leaving the dock at Westminster Park our course is at first along its northerly shore, a rocky bluff of some forty or fifty feet in height, upon whose summit may be seen some elegant residences but half hidden in the forest which crowns it. Doubling the Cape at the foot of Wells Island, we turn our prow in the direction of Alexandria Bay, of whose immense Hotels, especially the imposing front and tower of the Thousand Island House, we have at intervals caught sight, since rounding the lower end of Club Island, opposite Rockport. We get a distant view of several fine places to the eastward, which are on a cluster of small Islands known as "*the chain*," some of which are built upon and improved. The finest places are probably those of H. A. Packer, and Robert Packer, sons of the late Asa Packer, president of the Lehigh Valley R. R. and Coal company, and largely connected with the Coal and Iron interests of Pennsylvania. These gentlemen have expended large sums in building and beautifying their Islands. Among the ornamental structures is a very fine Iron bridge joining two of their Islands, under which the smaller class of our steam yachts pass freely, and which is reported to have cost not less than five thousand dollars.

The view of these places is however too distant to be perfectly satisfactory, unless as is sometimes the case, when time permits, Capt. Visger passes round that way to give his passengers an opportunity for a nearer inspection. In that case also we should find other and quite extensive improvements in the neighborhood, notably on "Summerland," the largest Island of this cluster. This, which contains about fifteen acres, has been purchased by a company of gentlemen mostly from Rochester, N. Y., who have already erected twelve or fifteen cottages, and more are in contemplation.

At our left as we pass up, and somewhat nigher than the "Chain" we get a good view of

FAIRY LAND,

an Island of some twenty acres, on which the Haydens, father and sons, of Columbus, Ohio, have made and are constantly adding to improvements upon their summer homes, of an extent and variety no where else surpassed in this vicinity. Three fine residences front the water, whose surroundings have been beautified with an untiring care, and at an expense which must have already reached far into the thousands. Boat houses, yacht houses and other conveniences for the enjoyment of life upon the river, are by the water side, while a fine tower for outlook, surmounted by a flag staff, crowns the summit, and windmills raise the water from the river into tanks, whence it is distributed for irrigating lawns, and the supply of every conceivable want.

Our trip now draws to a close. We pass nigh the foot of "Plantaganet," best known here as "Steamboat Island," on which is a small hunting and fishing lodge owned by A. E. Hume, Esq., an English gentleman of leisure and sporting tastes, who is said to have been somewhat engaged in business at Charleston, S. C., but who has for some years almost made his home in the vicinity of Alexandria Bay. Shortly beyond this we pass quite near enough for a good view of "Manhattan," Judge Spencer's elegant summer home, before referred to. We obtain a distant view of "Long Branch," owned by Mrs. Clark, of Watertown, who visits and entertains hosts of friends here, and nearer, of "Point Marguerite," the summer place of E. Anthony, Esq. The latter gentleman has here about twenty acres of land lying contiguous to the shore, where he indulges his taste for country life in directing the cultivation of garden and grounds. He is however, better known among photographic and picture men, as an early discoverer and successful operator in photography, and edits a monthly journal devoted to it. He probably made some of the first, perhaps the very first sun pictures ever produced in America. He is now the head of the oldest and most extensive house in the country for the supply of materials to that line of art. We pass quite near the light house and directly in front of "Bonnie Castle," landing in good time, and with an appetite sharpened for supper by the bracing and life giving breezes of the St. Lawrence.

The trip has given us all a rare and inexpensive treat, not soon to be forgotten, and we instinctively resolve to repeat it at the first favorable opportunity.

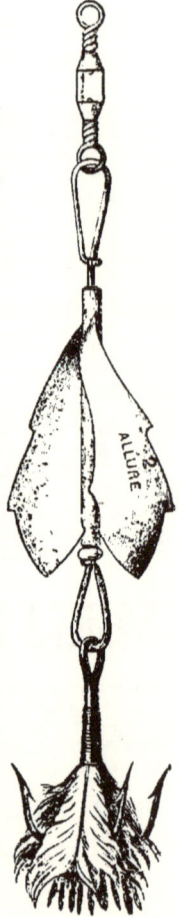